AF265737

LADIES IN TRAINING

Let's GET L.I.T.!!!!!

Authors: Cyvonne Gaines LCAS, Bennett Knightley, Connie Omari, LPC, NCC, Kehinde Watford JD, Sheila Wilson MA

DISCLAIMER

These materials are for educational purposes only and they are not intended to replace professional medical or legal advice

Dedication

Ladies in Training is a 501(c)(3) nonprofit organization whose mission is *to provide healing solutions to girls and their families in crisis*. This workbook is dedicated to every girl who dares to dream.

Table of Contents

Just Say No!

Substance Abuse Among Adolescents and Teens

Experimentation with alcohol and drugs during adolescence is common. Unfortunately, teenagers often don't see the link between their actions today and the consequences of tomorrow. They also have a tendency to feel indestructible and immune to the problems that others experience. Using alcohol and tobacco at a young age has negative health effects. Some teens will experiment and stop, or continue to use occasionally, without significant problems. Others will develop a dependency, moving on to more dangerous drugs and causing significant harm to themselves and possibly others. It is difficult to know which teens will experiment and stop and which will develop serious problems.

Who is at risk for developing serious problems???

Alcohol and drug use poses significant risks for the healthy development of adolescents. Using alcohol and drugs before the brain has fully developed increases your risk for future addiction to alcohol and drugs dramatically. Young people who start drinking alcohol before age 15 are 5 times more likely to develop alcohol abuse or dependence than people who first used alcohol at age 21 or older. Research for drug use and drug addiction has found similar results. Teenagers at risk for developing serious alcohol and drug problems include those:

• *with a family history of substance use disorders* - If you have a family history of alcoholism or addiction, you are four times more likely to develop a problem.
• *who are depressed*
• *who have low self-esteem,* and
• *who feel like they don't fit in or are out of the mainstream*

Alcohol is the most frequently used drug by teenagers in the United States. Significant statistics regarding alcohol use in teens include that about half of junior high and senior high school students drink alcohol on a monthly basis, and 14% of teens have been intoxicated at least once in the past year. Nearly 8% of teens who drink say they drink at least five or more alcoholic drinks in a row (binge drink).

What are the dangerous effects of alcohol use in teens???

Just a few of the many dangers of alcohol use in teens include the following:

• Alcohol decreases teens' ability to pay attention.

• Teens who have experienced alcohol withdrawal (hangover) tend to have difficulties with memory.
• The teenage brain that has been exposed to alcohol is at risk for being smaller in certain parts.
• In contrast to adults, teens tend to abuse alcohol with other substances, usually marijuana.
• The younger a person is when they begin drinking, the more likely they are to develop a problem with alcohol.

- Each year, almost 2,000 people under the age of 21 die in car crashes in which underage drinking is involved. Alcohol is involved in nearly half of all violent deaths involving youth.
- More than three times the number of eighth-grade girls who drink heavily said they have attempted suicide compared to girls in that grade who do not drink.
- Intoxication is associated with suicide attempts using more lethal methods, and positive blood alcohol levels are often found in people who complete suicide.
- Teens who drink are more likely to engage in sexual activity, have unprotected sex, have sex with a stranger, or be the victim or perpetrator of a sexual assault.
- Excess alcohol use can cause or mask other emotional problems, like anxiety or depression.
- Drinking in excess can lead to the use of other drugs, like marijuana, cocaine, or heroin.

Why do adolescents and teens use alcohol and drugs???

There is no one single reason why teenagers use drugs or alcohol. Here are some of the core issues and influences behind the behavior of teenage drug and alcohol use.

1. Other People. Teenagers see lots of people consuming various substances. They see their parents and other adults drinking alcohol, smoking cigarettes and, sometimes, trying other substances. Also, a teenager's social scene often revolves around drinking and smoking marijuana. Sometimes friends urge one another to have a drink or smoke pot, but it's just as common for teens to start trying a substance because it's readily available and they see all their friends enjoying it. In their minds, they see drug use as a part of the normal teenage experience.

2. Popular Media. Forty-five percent of teens agree with the statement: "The music that teens listen to makes marijuana seem cool." Forty-five percent of teens also agree with the statement "Movies and TV shows make drugs seem like an ok thing to do." So be aware of the media that you are consuming and talk to your parents, teachers and other trusted confidants.

3. Escape and Self-Medication. When teens are unhappy and can't find a healthy outlet for their frustration or a trusted confidant, they may turn to chemicals for solace. Depending on what substance they're trying, they may feel blissfully oblivious, wonderfully happy or energized and confident. The often tough teenage years can take an emotional toll on children, sometimes even causing depression, so when teens are given a chance to take something to make them feel better, many can't resist. For example, some teens abuse prescription medicine to manage stress or regulate their lives. Sometimes they abuse prescription stimulants (used to treat attention deficit hyperactivity disorder) to provide additional energy and the ability to focus when they're studying or taking tests. Others are abusing prescription pain relievers and tranquilizers to cope with academic, social or emotional stress.

4. Boredom. Teens who can't tolerate being alone, have trouble keeping themselves occupied or crave excitement are prime candidates for substance use. Not only do alcohol and marijuana give them something to do, but those substances help fill the internal void they feel. Further, they provide a common ground for interacting with like-minded teens, a way to instantly bond with a group of kids.

5. Rebellion. Different rebellious teens choose different substances to use based on their personalities. Alcohol is the drug of choice for the angry teenager because it frees him to behave aggressively. Methamphetamine, or meth, also encourages aggressive, violent behavior, and can be far more dangerous and potent than alcohol. Marijuana, on the other hand, often seems to reduce aggression and is more of an avoidance drug. Some teens abuse prescription medicine to party and get high. LSD and hallucinogens are also escape drugs, often used by young people who feel misunderstood and may long to escape to a more idealistic, kind world. Smoking cigarettes can be a form of rebellion to flaunt their independence and make their parents angry. The reasons for teenage drug-use are as complex as teenagers themselves.

6. Instant Gratification. Drugs and alcohol work quickly. The initial effects feel really good. Teenagers turn to drug use because they see it as a short-term shortcut to happiness.

7. Lack of Confidence. Many shy teenagers who lack confidence report that they'll do things under the influence of alcohol or drugs that they might not otherwise. This is part of the appeal of drugs and alcohol even for relatively self-confident teens; you have the courage to dance if you're a bad dancer, or sing at the top of your lungs even if you have a terrible voice, or kiss the girl you're attracted to. And alcohol and other drugs tend not only to loosen your inhibitions but to alleviate social anxiety. Not only do you have something in common with the other people around you, but there's the mentality that if you do anything or say anything stupid, everyone will just think you had too many drinks or smoked too much weed.

8. Misinformation. Perhaps the most avoidable cause of substance use is inaccurate information about drugs and alcohol. Nearly every teenager has friends who claim to be experts on various recreational substances, and they're happy to assure her that the risks are minimal. Educate your teenagers about drug use, so they get the real facts about the dangers of drug use.

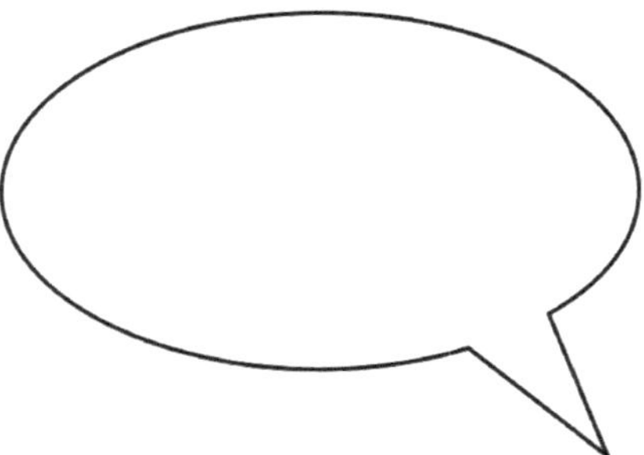

If you're using, or thinking of using drugs or alcohol, it's important to remember that there are other options besides drugs and alcohol. One of the most important things you can do is see your *school counselor.* Talking to someone other than friends and family can give you a fresh perspective and teach you new ways to cope with your feelings. Talk to your parents, doctors, teachers, or other adults about options that are affordable (or free) in your school or neighborhood. Exercise is a great way to get your body to produce some of the natural chemicals (called endorphins) that make you feel better all over and help reduce the effects of stress. Something as simple as going for a run or long walk can have amazing effects on how you feel. In addition to the short-term benefits, in the long run, exercise will give you more energy and help you feel good about your body. Making the time to learn something new is another way to give your mind something to do. Make a list of things you're interested in and go check out some books from the library to become an expert! Getting involved in art can be an inexpensive way to relax and express your creativity. All you need is paper, a pencil, and your ideas to become an artist, poet, or songwriter.

It's not always easy to "just say no" when it comes to alcohol and drugs. There can be many pressures to use, particularly in social situations or when hanging out with friends who use. Although real friends won't care whether you use drugs or alcohol or not, sometimes it helps to have responses prepared in case other people feel like pressuring you. Some creative ways to refuse include:
· I'm on probation and have to pass a drug test tomorrow
· I've got a math (or English, or social studies . . .) final tomorrow that I can't risk failing
· I'm allergic to alcohol
· I have only one lung… when in doubt, use humor—and always remember, it's your choice, not theirs...

Alcoholism and drug dependence are not moral issues, are not a matter of choice, or a lack of willpower. While saying no is not always easy, it is, by far, the better choice!

Love Me Or Leave Me

There are three different types of relationships.

Dating   Family   Social or Friendship

Healthy relationships contain a good balance of conflict and good times.

Healthy relationships are:

- Respectful
- Supportive
- Filled with appreciation
- Open Communication

# Warning signs of a bad relationship…

- Healthy relationships are not:
    - Abusive (physical, emotional, verbal, or sexual)
    - Formed by Oppression, Force or Bullying
        - Examples include the following:
            - Guilt – "You should do this if you really care for me"
            - Shaming - "You wouldn't dress that way if you didn't want people to think you were a slut."
            - Manipulation – "No one else can treat you better than me."
            - Lying, tricking, or deceit - A boy telling a girl that if they have sex with you, they will become your boyfriend, knowing that the boy has no intentions of doing so.
            - Bullying - " if you don't give me your lunch I'm going to beat you up."
    - Disrespectful - " you are too fat and ugly to be my friend."

Vignette: Shantay

Shantay and Deion have been seeing each other. Deion began to share that he has feelings for Shantay. Shantay enjoys hanging out with Deion but does not feel the same way. She isn't sure what to do or say.

What can Shantay do?

1. Tell Deion that she enjoys hanging out with him but does not want to be more than friends.

____

____

____

____

____

____

2. Avoid saying anything. He can figure it out.

3. Tell your home girl to let him know.

4. Tell Deion that you feel the same way and try to figure out what to do later.

Communication

- Clear communication is being honest and clearly stating what you are thinking.
- All relationships require communication. There's many ways to communicate.
- Speaking up helps to start conversations.
- Healthy relationships have to have clear and strong communication in order to be successful.
- Communication can be easy and also really difficult. Especially if you do not want to be hurtful. When in doubt try being honest.

Scenario

Arianna has been talking to Jay and she think she is in love with him. You know that Jay is a player and saw him kissing another girl at the movies. How should a strong communicator deal with this?

1. Don't tell, it's not your business

____
____
____
____
____
____

2. Definitely tell her, she needs to know he's playing around.

____

____

____

____

3. Talk to Jay and demand that he confess to your friend.

____

____

____

____

4. Try and hint to your friend without being direct about it because it's not your business.

____

____

____

____

____

HEALTHY RELATIONSHIPS

•Healthy relationships start within.
•Having a positive view of yourself will make all of your relationships better.
•Practice identifying 3 things about yourself that you like and can begin to celebrate.
•Here's a start: You are an intelligent Lady in Training! Help your neighbor if they cannot find anything about themselves that is special.

Example 2: Shantay

Shantay and Ayanna both like the same person. Instantly there are bad feelings between Shantay and Ayanna. They start to send each other mean messages on social media. Over time, they develop a really bad relationship with each other. They want to get out some of their negative feelings toward each other and to hurt each other.

What are some other options?

____

____

____

____

____

____

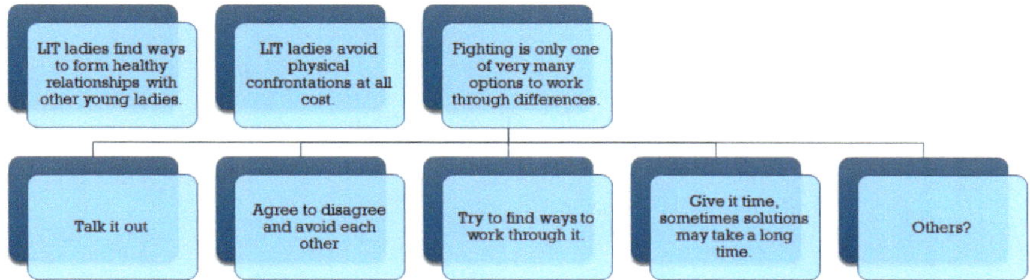

LIT ladies find ways to form healthy relationships with other young ladies.
LIT ladies avoid physical confrontations at all cost.
Fighting is only one of very many options to work through differences.
Talk it out
Agree to disagree and avoid each other
Try to find ways to work through it.
Give it time, sometimes solutions may take a long time.
Others?

Feeling Myself

We live in a society that attempts to make girls feel guilty for feeling confident in themselves. For instance, if a girl thinks highly of herself, discouragement often follows and can be seen in comments such as, " she think she's all that." As a result, many young girls face extreme insecurities, where they lack confidence in themselves. Low confidence leads to poor self and body image, unhealthy relationships, and choosing not to reach one's actual potential for fear of coming off as rude or arrogant. And while thinking higher of yourself than you do of other people is off-putting, most girls are not striving to think higher of themselves than others, but simply highly of themselves. I am here to enforce the fact that we all should think highly of ourselves, because it's through that self image that we can all reach a maximum potential.

Ladies in Training, no matter what your shape, your size, your skin complexion, your hair texture, length, or thickness is…You. Are. Beautiful. You have to believe this.

If you cannot believe that you are beautiful, it does not matter what you do to yourself, it will not become true for you. People tend to be able to do what they think they can do. Self-efficacy, the term coined by Bandura in Bandura, 1982, means that a person will do what they believe they are capable of achieving. If a person does not believe that he or she can be successful at something, they are likely not going to be. For instance, a doctor can only become a doctor if they think they have what it takes to become a doctor. The same applies for beauty. You're only as beautiful as you think you can be; think positively and reflect the beauty that is inside of each and every one of you.

To assist you with this process, I would like to introduce the concept of, "act as if" - a technique that will be used throughout this journey. It was introduced to me during the beginning of my professional career. I was experiencing a relatively difficult time with being a counselor, especially when working with people who were older than me. During supervision, my supervisor confronted my insecurities along this domain. Though she acknowledge my difficulties, she reinforced the fact that it was my job to provide psychotherapy to the clients who were assigned to me, even those who were older. Basically, she told me that if I wanted my job, I had to be willing to overcome what I thought to be "taboo," which was exerting authority over people who were chronologically older than me. In response to her feedback, I made the following comment: "but I don't know how to find the confidence to counsel people who are older than me." The response she gave was magnificent. She validated my insecurity and stated, "it's OK not to know how to do it, but "act as if," you do." In other words, I did not have to know how to be a good counselor to be a good counselor as long as I acted as if I was a good counselor. In this case, Ladies in Training, you can learn to "act as if" you are beautiful, and in essence the beauty within you will shine brightly to be seen and admired by yourself and others. Keep this in mind as you develop your style.

One way you can "act as if" you are beautiful inside is to ensure that your presentation reflects beauty. I cannot tell you how many clients come into my office with insecurities about the lack of beauty that they feel of themselves while wearing sweatpants and a T-shirt! Presentation means everything when we want to feel beautiful. Make sure you take the appropriate time to groom yourself, wear clean fitted clothing, and makeup your face for the way that is beautiful to you. I am not asking that you spend an arm and a leg to fulfill this goal, and I certainly do not expect you to be overcome with time consuming beauty strategies. However, make sure you present yourself in such a way that will reflect the message you wish to convey. If you want me to think you are beautiful, I need you to first think you are beautiful. Also, please note that treating yourself in a beautiful manner is not the same as wearing skirts and shorts that show your panties.

What can you change about your appearance that will cause you to "act as if?

____

____

____

____

____

____

Another way to "act as if" you are beautiful is to get a massage. Massages are great ways to bring awareness to our bodies because many of us take our bodies for granted. Thus, it is hard to appreciate something you rarely acknowledge. By getting a massage, you force yourself to know more about your body by appreciating the feelings that touch brings to it. If a massage is out of your price range, do not despair. There are other ways you can bring the feeling of positive touch into your life. As a matter of fact, any drugstore has self-massage equipment that can be purchased relatively inexpensively. Another way to receive a massage is through the connections with people that you already have. Do not be afraid to ask for a massage as a favor from a significant other, close friend, or family member. Also you can find creative ways to receive massages. For me, it is cheaper to get a manicure or a pedicure then purchase a massage, so I only frequent salons that have massage chairs. That way, I get a massage and pedicure for the same price! By being kind to yourself in the way a massage can be, you are "acting as if" you are beautiful.

How can you incorporate the idea of a massage or the concept of touch into your life in order to "act as if" you are beautiful?

____

____

____

____

____

____

Ladies in Training, you can also "act as if" you are beautiful by changing your diet and exercising. This is not intended to be a hypocritical statement that now reinforces the need to be petite to be beautiful, but an important component to beauty is being healthy. By eating better and exercising more, your body will naturally become

healthier and increase the production of hormones associated with pleasurable feelings. Other benefits of maintaining a healthy diet and exercise routine include having clearer skin, healthy your hair, and stronger nails. All these elements will enhance your natural beauty.

What changes can you make to your diet and exercise in order to " act as if"?

____

____

____

____

____

____

Another way you can "act as if" you are beautiful is to have a date night. Having a date night includes setting aside a time to do something you enjoy. While this can be done with a partner, I encourage doing your date night alone. I am encouraging a solo date night because this is an attempt to do exactly what you want to do, to make you feel better. You will almost always sacrifice some level of comfort for doing things with someone else and the purpose of having this date night is to empower yourself. Examples of date nights can include going to the library, going to a basketball or football game, or watching a movie. Whatever brings happiness and peace to you should be incorporated into your date night. By "acting as if" you are beautiful in this regard, you'll certainly be encouraged to feel more beautiful about yourself.

What challenges do you anticipate experiencing in the implementation of the "act as if" technique?

____

____

____

____

What is your plan of action for overcoming the challenges you anticipate in the "act as if"
technique?

____

____

____

____

____

____

I Could Never Do That

Please read the subtitle of the section out loud and to yourself again. Again. Again. And again.
Now let that be the last time you ever say or think that statement for the rest of your life. It is
unfortunate that we live in a world that not only causes us to question self-confidence regarding
our external ourselves but causes us to lack self confidence in our internal selves as well.
Females are particularly vulnerable to feelings of poor self-confidence because we are socialized
to meet the needs of others. Thus, if we are not contributing to others in the way that we are
expected or if we receive negative feedback about ourselves, we internalize these feelings which
foster an environment for self-doubt and insecurity.

What messages have you been told regarding your inability to achieve certain goals?

____

____

____

____

____

Let's review an example of when I learned the importance of self-confidence. As an undergraduate student in 2004, I had the opportunity to study abroad in Cape Town South Africa. As part of our requirement, we were expected to write weekly papers on different topics we covered on our trip. The papers were graded by our teaching assistant. Despite the teaching assistant's ability to thrive academically, his social skills were inadequate. After a review of one of my papers, he made the following statement towards me, "you will never get into graduate school writing like that." Despite the fact that I was able to attend a prestigious undergraduate school and was invited to participate in a (honors) study abroad program which vouched for my credibility for academic success, I allowed his one opinion to dictate how I felt about myself. I internalize his feedback, and I strongly believed that by doing so these thoughts contributed to the fact that I was denied by 14 different graduate schools before I eventually gained admission for a doctorate degree.

Where did I go wrong? I let my teaching assistant who clearly did not have my best interest at heart determine my fate. This is something many of us find ourselves doing, even though we know better. We must understand that unfortunately people say and do things to hurt us, but we cannot let those feelings dictate how we perceive ourselves. By empowering ourselves and being responsible for our own fate. We remain in control.

Believe it or not, a lot of our negative beliefs about ourselves occur because we often feel attacked by others when the people that we presume to be attacking us do not intend to. In fact, my mother always told me but if you could have four to five relationships that withstand these communication challenges, consider yourself lucky. The issue within these conflicts is not that offensive people are heartless and intentionally want us to feel bad (at least most of them do not). Instead, people are caught up in their own lives, concerned about the way they do things, and surrounded by what is important to them and do not realize how what they're saying or doing impacts others.

I'm not sure how you feel about my teaching assistant, but I honestly feel as if his intent was to motivate me to do better. Previously, I had spoken about wanting to attend graduate school with him. He thought I submitted a paper that he felt demonstrated poor scholarly performance and had concerns about my ability to be successful and decided to share them with me. The way he presented this concern, however, was damaging to my self-confidence, but it was up to me to rectify the situation, not him. Though it took me a while to understand this, rather than allow his perception of me to dictate how I felt about myself, I eventually choose to see the brighter perspective and used that experience as a moment of empowerment. Because I was able to turn his feedback into something motivating, I was able to become empowered.

Identify a time when you were mistreated. How can you redefine your perceptions of the motives of the person who mistreated you and develop the confidence that you need to be empowered?

Know Your Rights

Overview

- A minor is an unmarried person under 18 years of age.
- Minors have **most** of the same constitutional rights as adults.
- Regardless of citizenship you have the following Constitutional rights:
- **1st Amendment** Freedom of Speech
- **4th Amendment** Freedom from unreasonable search and seizure
- **5th Amendment** Freedom from self-incrimination (aka the right to remain silent)

Freedom of Speech

Have you ever been told to be quiet? Identify reasons that freedom of speech is important.

____
____
____
____
____
____

The First Amendment protects freedom of speech in school. Schools may not punish students for saying something just because it is controversial, such as discussing topics like school segregation, teen pregnancy, gay rights, war, and politics. It also protects symbolic speech, such as t-shirts, buttons, flags, decals. Peaceful demonstrations such as picketing or marching are protected as long as it does not disrupt school.

There are limits! Not all speech is protected by the Constitution. Speech that is vulgar, lewd, or disruptive is not protected. Other unprotected speech includes:
1. True threats
2. Defamatory
3. Obscene
4. Inciting riots or violence
5. Promotes illegal activities
6. Interferes with appropriate discipline in the school.

Flyers and Written Materials

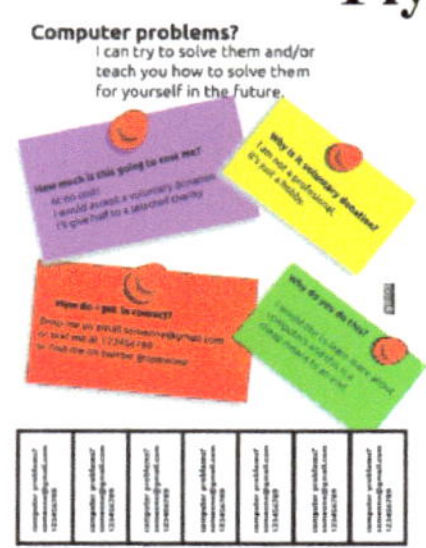

Students have a right to bring and distribute flyers and other written materials to school without permission. Your school can limit when, where, and how the materials are distributed. **BEWARE!!!** If flyers and written materials contain the prohibited speech mentioned above, then you can get in trouble for distributing them.

Internet Speech

You have the right to free speech when emailing, blogging, creating a website, or posting information on a website. It is mandatory to follow school rules when using school computers on campus. You can be punished for off-campus internet speech that has a direct and immediate impact on the safety or orderly operation of the school.

Flag Salute and Pledge of Allegiance

You do not have to stand for nor say the Pledge of Allegiance. Your school may not force you to say the Pledge of Allegiance and may not punish you for refusing to do so. Your school can not require you to explain why you do not want to salute the flag or say the Pledge of Allegiance.

Freedom from Unreasonable Search and Seizure

What does it mean, to you, to be protected from unreasonable search and seizure in class and at school?

____
____
____
____

The Fourth Amendment protects your privacy from government intrusion. You have a **right** to be free from unreasonable searches of your person and seizure of your belongings.

School Officials

School officials and school resource officers may only search you or your belongings if they have "reasonable suspicion" to believe that you have something illegal or something that is not allowed at school. Reasonable suspicion MUST be based on specific, articulable facts that something illegal has happened, is happening, or will happen. It can not be based on a guess, hunch, or generalized suspicion. It is important to note, however, **school officials can search lockers, school computers, and other school property for any reason.**

Outside Law Enforcement

An outside law enforcement officer must have "probable cause" to conduct a search or requests a school official to conduct a search. This is a higher standard than the "reasonable suspicion" required by school officials. Probable cause means that there is specific evidence of a "substantial chance" that the student has something unauthorized or illegal. If there is no probable cause and you do not give consent for the search, then the search is illegal.

Search and Seizure

Why must officials and officers be careful in following the rules about searches and seizures?

____

____

____

____

Consent

You have a right to say no to school officials and law enforcement officers who ask for permission to conduct a search of you or your belongings. If you say "no," the search MUST not happen unless there is reasonable suspicion or probable cause for the search.

"I DO NOT CONSENT TO THIS SEARCH" must be said out loud. Your silence indicates that you consent or agree to what they are doing.

Search Warrants

If you do not consent to the search, Officers can seek search warrants from the court to search and seize evidence of a crime. They must have probable cause to get a search warrant. With a search warrant, the police can enter your home without permission even if you are not present.

Typically your property can not be seized without a search warrant. There are, however, exceptions to the warrant requirement which include:
1. When the officer is searching for weapons within a wingspan
2. Emergencies such as a hot pursuit
3. When the item is in plain view
4. Under the Patriot Act

If, during a search, a school official or law enforcement officer finds something that is illegal or against school rules, they can take it from you. Any evidence that is seized can be used against you in a delinquency or criminal proceeding and in a school disciplinary hearing.

The Right to Remain Silent

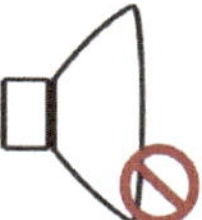

The Fifth Amendment protects against self-incrimination. It gives every person the right to not answer questions asked by a police officer or government agent. You have a right to be free from self-incrimination. In other words, you do not have to tell on yourself when you are suspected of committing a crime or when charged with a crime.

Miranda Warnings

(This is NOT an episode of Law and Order. They do not have to read you your rights when placing you under arrest.)

Any student under the age of 18 who is "in custody" (i.e., detained or under arrest), with a law enforcement officer (including a school resource officer) **MUST** be given, **before questioning**, his/her Miranda warnings:

1. You have the right to remain silent;
2. Any statement made by you can be used against you in court;
3. You have the right to have an attorney present during questioning;
4. If you can't afford an attorney, one will be appointed before any questioning if you want.
5. You may stop questioning at any time and ask for an attorney.
6. You have the right to have a parent, guardian, or custodian, present during questioning. (**ALWAYS** ask to have your parent present at **ALL** times when being questioned by the police or any adult)

If a student is age 13 or younger, an admission or confession can **NOT** be used against the student in court unless the confession or admission was made in the presence of the student's parent, guardian, custodian, or attorney. A student who is age 13 or younger cannot give up the requirement of having a parent, guardian, or custodian present.

For students over the age of 13, if the student chooses to make statement while in custody, there is no legal requirement for a parent, guardian, or custodian to be present. The student **MUST** be informed of their right to have a parent, guardian, or custodian, as well as an attorney, present.

Regardless of age, "in custody" interrogations by law enforcement officers **MUST** stop if the student indicates they do not want to be questioned any more.

DO NOT BE AFRAID
TO DEMAND YOUR RIGHTS!

I said NO!!!
How Much Do You Know About Sexual Assault?

The definition of sexual assault is an illegal sexual contact that usually involves force upon a person without consent or is inflicted upon a person who is incapable of giving consent (as because of age or physical or mental incapacity) or who places the assailant (such as a doctor) in a position of trust or authority.

To examine your understanding of sexual assault, please take this quiz by circling true or false and compare them to the answers at the end of this chapter.

1. Rape is about sexual gratification.   T   F

2. Sex crimes, including sexual harassment and frottage, are crimes of passion or desire. T   F

3. Men can be sexually assaulted.   T   F

4. Most sexual assaults are interracial – the perpetrator and victim are different races.   T   F

5. Rapes are rarely reported to the police.   T   F

6. The way a woman is dressed or the fact that she is drunk is often why she is raped.   T   F

7. Sexual offenders are many times known by the victim.   T   F

8. When a woman says "no" she really means "maybe" or "yes".   T   F

9. Spouses cannot sexually assault each other.   T   F

10. Ugly, old or disabled people are never sexually assaulted.   T   F

11. Victims who have been sexually assaulted may be very calm and controlled.   T   F

12. The culture of violence that we live in contributes to sexual violence.   T   F

13. Men can't help themselves. Once they are sexually aroused, they cannot stop.   T   F

14. Sexual harassment is a form of sexual assault.   T   F

15. Only gay men are raped, and they are only raped by other gay men.   T   F

16. Gay women can be victims of sexual assault.   T   F

17. Rapes only occur by strangers in dark alleys.   T   F

18. Women always lie about sexual assault to save their reputation or get revenge on a ex-partner.   T   F

19. Weapons, including guns, knives and fists, are often used to intimidate sexual assault victims.   T   F

20. If a person willingly goes to someone's room or house or goes to a bar, she/he assumes the risk of sexual assault. The perpetrator can't be blamed for anything that happens.   T   F

How Much Do You Know About Sexual Assault?

The Answers

FALSE 1. Rape is about sexual gratification.
Sexual assault is a violent assault acted out in a sexual way. It is about power and control.

FALSE 2. Sex crimes are crimes of passion or desire.
Sex crimes are crimes of violence, anger and power, not passion or sexual gratification.

TRUE 3. Men can be sexually assaulted.
Men are victims of sexual assault. It is estimated that 1 out of 10 men will be sexually assaulted either by another male or a female during his lifetime.

FALSE 4. Most sexual assaults are interracial– the perpetrator and victim are different races
.
In the majority of sexual assaults the victim and the perpetrator are of the same race. Caucasian victims are most common, then African-Americans, Hispanics, and people identifying themselves as other, such as Asian or Native American. This debunks the myth that people of color are the primary perpetrators of sexual assault – or the primary victims.
TRUE 5. Rapes are rarely reported to the police.
The crime of rape is usually not reported to the police. Rape is an under-reported crime in the United States. It is estimated that for every rape reported to the police, 7-10 rapes are not reported.

FALSE 6. The way a woman is dressed or the fact that she is drunk is often why she is raped.
Sexual assault is not the result of the way a person dresses or acts. It is the assailant who decides to assault another individual. The victim is not an accessory to the crime. Being intoxicated may make a victim more vulnerable for an assault, but nothing and no one is responsible for an assault but a perpetrator. After all, do we say this about victims of other types of crimes? Do we say to a man who has been mugged – what were you doing wearing that suit? Why were you downtown? What made you get money out of the ATM machine in that location? Didn't you think a briefcase would signal your availability to a criminal?

TRUE 7. Sexual offenders are many times known by the victim.
Most sexual assaults are committed by someone the victim knows. Studies show that approximately 80% of the people reporting sexual assaults knew their assailants.

FALSE 8. When a woman says "no" she really means "maybe" or "yes".
When a woman or a man says "no," he or she means "no." "No" means no. Sexual intercourse without consent is rape. A person has the right to control his or her own body.

FALSE 9. Spouses cannot sexually assault each other.

Spouses can and do sexually assault each other, and it is a crime in NJ. Marital status does not give either partner the right to have sexual intercourse without the other spouse's consent. This includes having sex with your partner while they are asleep or intoxicated, or forcing or pressuring them to perform a sexual act they are not comfortable with.

FALSE 10. Ugly, old or disabled people are never sexually assaulted.
The myth that only young, pretty women are sexually assaulted stems from the myth that sexual assault is based on sex and physical attraction. Sexual assault is a crime of power and control and offenders often choose people whom they perceive as most vulnerable to attack or over whom they believe they can assert power.

TRUE 11. Victims who have been sexually assaulted may be very calm and controlled.
Victims of sexual assault exhibit a spectrum of responses to the assault which can include: calm, hysteria, withdrawal, anger, apathy, denial and shock. Being sexually assaulted is a very traumatic experience and reactions to the assault and the length of time needed to process through the experience vary with each person. There is no "right way" to react to being sexually assaulted.

TRUE 12. The culture of violence that we live in contributes to sexual violence.
Anytime women are objectified or sexualized, this contributes to a culture that tolerates and promotes sexual violence. Anytime there is discrimination or stereotyping based on race, gender, sexual orientation, or abilities, anytime an excuse is found for why someone is found lacking, not equal or less than, it contributes to a culture that allows perpetrators to see those victims as less than human beings and disposable.

FALSE 13. Men can't help themselves. Once they are sexually aroused, they cannot stop.
Forcing sexual activity without consent is a choice on the part of the perpetrator. Rape is an aggressive and violent act. Sex is used as the most effective way of degrading the victim, and the act is more about feeding the perpetrator's need for power than sexual gratification. After all, if a man was having sex (with a consenting partner!) and the other person's parent walked through the room – would he stop? Yeah, he would stop, and grab his clothes, and jump out the window, probably.

TRUE 14. Sexual harassment is a form of sexual assault. Sexual assault ranges from sexual harassment, including unsolicited sexually explicit words or physical contact, to peeping, flashing, "dry humping," oral sex and penetration. Sexual assault is any sexual act without the consent of the victim.

FALSE 15. Only gay men are raped, and they are only raped by other gay men.
Heterosexual and homosexual men are raped, and rapists can be heterosexual or homosexual. Men(as well as women) are raped because they are vulnerable based on factors such as age, isolation or status. They are often raped as part of a violent attack that is aimed at domination and degradation.

TRUE 16. Gay women can be victims of sexual assault. All men and all women, girls and boys, regardless of age, gender, race, status or sexual orientation, can be victims of sexual assault.

FALSE 17. Rapes only occur by strangers in dark alleys. A majority of rapes occur in residences. Most rapes occur in or near a victim's residence or near a friend or relative's home. This is consistent with the fact that 80% of victims knew their perpetrator before the sexual assault.

FALSE 18. Women always lie about sexual assault to save their reputation or get revenge on a ex-partner. Sexual assault is a vastly underreported crime. Women are more likely to lie and say they haven't been sexually assaulted, out of shame or fear of further assaults or harassment. According to the FBI, false allegations of rapes are no greater than those of other crimes – typically about 2%. The SANE/SART process is a complicated and involved process, and that usually deters false reporting as well.

FALSE 19. Weapons, such as guns, knives and fists, are often used to intimidate rape victims. The offender often uses physical strength, physical violence, intimidation, and threats to overpower a victim. More often than actual weapons, perpetrators often uses the victim's trust developed through their relationship, even short term relationships, to create an opportunity to commit the sexual assault. The offender may have intimate knowledge about the victim's life, such as where he/she works, where he/she goes to school or information about his/her family and friends. This enhances the credibility of any threats made by the offender since he has the knowledge about his/her life to carry them out.

FALSE 20. If a person willingly goes to someone's room or house or goes to a bar, she/he assumes the risk of sexual assault. The perpetrator can't be blamed for anything that happens. This "assumption of risk" wrongfully places the responsibility of the offender's actions with the victim. Even if a person went voluntarily to someone's residence or room and consented to engage in some sexual activity, it does not serve as blanket consent for all sexual activity. If a person is unsure about whether the other person is comfortable with an elevated level of sexual activity, the person should stop and ask. When someone says "no" or "stop" that means STOP. Sexual activity forced upon another without consent is sexual assault. This skewered logic is used to justify the actions of Kobe Bryant, the Duke Lacrosse players, and many other sexual assaults.

Autobiographies

Cyvonne Gaines LCAS

Cyvonne Gaines is licensed as a Licensed Chemical Addictions Specialist, where she specializes in Substance Abuse Treatment. Born and raised in a small town in North Carolina, Cyvonne was a pioneer of her time. She was one of the first African Americans within her community to co-educate alongside her white counterparts during the Jim Crow Era. Having initially begun this experience by having to sit in the back of the classroom and be referred to as "The Colored Girl," Cyvonne advocated for equality in conjunction with racial integration. One of Cyvonne's biggest accomplishments of the time, was advocating for, and ultimately winning the battle to integrate the cheerleading squad. Cyvonne later represented her high school as the Maid of Honor for homecoming.

Cyvonne's desire to embark upon change exceeded far beyond her hometown. Cyvonne received a BA in Early Childhood Education at the University of N.C. and a Masters in Special Education with an emphasis on the emotionally handicapped at N.C. Central University. Cyvonne taught within the public school systems of NC and Texas for 16 years in both the traditional and special needs population.

In 2007, Cyvonne transitioned from the education to the mental health field. After having hands on experience as a substance abuse counselor and Qualified Professional, Cyvonne became the Assistant and Clinical Director of a N.C. mental health agency, where she worked until the agency closed its doors in 2012.

With her wealth of knowledge and compassion for the substance abusing field, in 2013, Cyvonne became the Owner and Operator of Gaining Ground LLC, located in Wadesboro N.C. Here, Cyvonne provides DWI and other substance abuse services, including but not limited to DWI assessments, Alcohol Drug Education Traffic School (ADETS), DWI classes, and out of state DWI Reviews.

Connie Omari LPC, NCC

Connie is a licensed professional counselor and national certified counselor. Connie's theoretical orientation is dialectical behavior therapy (DBT), which is an evidence-based practice that emphasizes the concepts of mindfulness, distress tolerance, interpersonal effectiveness, as well as emotional regulation techniques. Connie utilizes her practice in DBT to conceptualize common themes inherent in young women and girls and inspire them to engage in their own thought-provoking, spiritually motivating, and empowering journeys. Connie then trained her staff of Sacred Journey Inc. (partial hospitalization for women) and Zynna's Place (transitional for women) to do the same.

Connie received her bachelor of arts from the University of North Carolina at Chapel Hill in psychology and African American studies. As a college student, Connie traveled internationally to broaden her scope of understanding of the unique challenges inherent in minority communities across the globe. Connie's philanthropic experiences were mainly fixated on the African Diaspora and included Ghana, West Africa; Cape Town, South Africa; Ocho Rios, Jamaica, and Presidio Beach, Brazil. After college, Connie received her master of arts and master of education from Teachers College, Columbia University, where Connie majored in psychological counseling with an emphasis on multiculturalism. Connie completed her doctorate of philosophy from Regent University in counselor education and supervision in 2017.

Connie's compassion for mental health and minority affairs is deeply rooted in her childhood. Connie was raised in the small town of Norwood, NC, a quiet community in the southeastern part of the United States. It was here that Connie first became aware of the adversity imposed upon disadvantaged people as Connie observed various levels of overt, cultural and institutionalized forms of oppression within my community. Utilizing a culturally sensitive and spiritually inclined awareness, Connie combines her experience with oppression, her professional training, and her international observations to use her voice to challenge institutional norms and provide empowerment for women and girls around the world. Connie's specialty includes assisting women with the following challenges: poor body image and self-image, addictive behaviors, poor conflict resolution skills, trauma history related to domestic and sexual violence, and healthy relationships.

Kehinde Watford JD

Kehinde Watford is a licensed criminal attorney and certified mediator. She received her Bachelor of Science in Criminal Justice at East Carolina University in 2003 and her Juris Doctor from North Carolina Central University School of Law in 2006.

Kehinde has maintained a solo law practice in Durham, NC focusing primarily in the areas of criminal defense and family law since 2006. She is currently a volunteer with Legal Aid's "Lawyer on the Line", advisor for the North Carolina Racial Equity Network, and a member of Zeta Phi Beta Sorority, Inc.

She has extensive leadership experience having held executive board positions within numerous organizations. Her focus on community collaboration has also led her to a number of volunteer opportunities and community leadership roles. In her downtime, Kehinde enjoys traveling, shopping, scrapbooking, bowling, and spending time with her family.

Sheila Wilson MA

Sheila E. Wilson has been providing violence prevention services for women and children for over 10 years. In her role as a Community Outreach Educator Ms. Wilson provided direct family support services. Through the coordination and implementation of support services Ms. Wilson assisted with stabilizing families impacted by complex medical and environmental circumstances. In her role of providing violence prevention program to women, Ms. Wilson has conducted numerous anti-violence workshops for the past three years at the Hudson County Corrections and Secaucus Juvenile Detention Centers in New Jersey. She has also been a Confidential Sexual Assault Advocate for over 9 years. Ms. Wilson holds a B.A. in Political Science and a M.A. in Sociology and Social Justice. She has 15 years of professional experience including paralegal duties in both state and federal capacities. She also has experience in research and investigation and has worked as a legal analyst in the government and private sector.

9 781986 648387